50 Taste of Spain Dishes

By: Kelly Johnson

Table of Contents

- Paella Valenciana
- Tortilla Española
- Gazpacho
- Patatas Bravas
- Gambas al Ajillo
- Pisto Manchego
- Albondigas
- Fabada Asturiana
- Pollo al Ajillo
- Calamares a la Romana
- Escalivada
- Bacalao al Pil Pil
- Churros con Chocolate
- Jamón Ibérico Croquettes
- Empanada Gallega
- Salmorejo
- Arroz Negro
- Pulpo a la Gallega
- Tarta de Santiago
- Espinacas con Garbanzos
- Lentejas a la Riojana
- Fideuà
- Cocido Madrileño
- Caldereta de Cordero
- Chistorra al Vino
- Huevos a la Flamenca
- Ensalada Rusa
- Merluza a la Koskera
- Rabo de Toro
- Callos a la Madrileña
- Zarzuela de Pescado
- Migas Extremeñas
- Pimientos del Piquillo Rellenos
- Conejo al Salmorejo
- Boquerones en Vinagre

- Berenjenas con Miel
- Chuletas de Cordero a la Manchega
- Almejas a la Marinera
- Arroz con Leche
- Solomillo al Whisky
- Paté de Cabracho
- Cordero Asado a la Segoviana
- Chanfaina
- Bacalao a la Vizcaína
- Chorizo a la Sidra
- Leche Frita
- Mejillones al Vapor
- Revuelto de Setas
- Tumbet
- Torrijas

Paella Valenciana

Ingredients:

- 2 cups short-grain rice (e.g., Bomba)
- 4 cups chicken or seafood stock
- 1/2 lb chicken, cut into small pieces
- 1/2 lb rabbit, cut into small pieces
- 1/2 cup green beans (flat variety)
- 1/4 cup lima beans
- 1 large tomato, grated
- 2 cloves garlic, minced
- 1/4 cup olive oil
- 1/2 teaspoon saffron threads, soaked in warm water
- 1 teaspoon smoked paprika
- Salt and freshly ground black pepper

Instructions:

1. **Prepare the Pan:** Heat olive oil in a large paella pan over medium heat. Brown the chicken and rabbit pieces. Remove and set aside.
2. **Cook Vegetables:** In the same pan, sauté green beans and lima beans until tender.
3. **Add Garlic and Tomato:** Stir in garlic and grated tomato. Cook for 2-3 minutes, then add smoked paprika.
4. **Add Rice:** Add the rice to the pan and toast for 2 minutes, stirring constantly.
5. **Add Stock and Saffron:** Pour in the stock and saffron-infused water. Return the chicken and rabbit to the pan.
6. **Simmer:** Reduce heat and simmer for 20-25 minutes, without stirring, until the liquid is absorbed.
7. **Serve:** Let rest for a few minutes before serving.

Tortilla Española

Ingredients:

- 6 large eggs
- 4 medium potatoes, peeled and thinly sliced
- 1 medium onion, thinly sliced
- 1/2 cup olive oil
- Salt

Instructions:

1. **Cook Potatoes and Onions:** Heat olive oil in a large skillet. Add potatoes and onions, cooking until tender. Drain and season with salt.
2. **Mix with Eggs:** In a bowl, beat the eggs and mix with the cooked potatoes and onions.
3. **Cook the Tortilla:** Return the mixture to the skillet, cooking over medium heat until the bottom is set. Flip and cook the other side until fully set.
4. **Serve:** Slice into wedges and serve warm or at room temperature.

Gazpacho

Ingredients:

- 6 ripe tomatoes
- 1 cucumber, peeled and chopped
- 1 green bell pepper, chopped
- 1 small red onion, chopped
- 2 cloves garlic
- 3 cups tomato juice
- 1/4 cup olive oil
- 2 tablespoons red wine vinegar
- Salt and freshly ground black pepper
- Croutons, for garnish

Instructions:

1. **Blend Ingredients:** Combine all vegetables, garlic, olive oil, and vinegar in a blender. Blend until smooth.
2. **Chill:** Refrigerate for at least 2 hours.
3. **Serve:** Garnish with croutons and serve cold.

Patatas Bravas

Ingredients:

- 4 medium potatoes, peeled and cubed
- 1/4 cup olive oil
- 1 cup tomato sauce
- 1 teaspoon smoked paprika
- 1/4 teaspoon cayenne pepper
- Salt
- Fresh parsley, chopped (for garnish)

Instructions:

1. **Fry Potatoes:** Heat olive oil in a skillet. Fry the potatoes until golden and crispy. Drain and season with salt.
2. **Make Sauce:** Heat tomato sauce in a small saucepan. Stir in paprika and cayenne pepper. Simmer for 5 minutes.
3. **Serve:** Drizzle sauce over the potatoes and garnish with parsley.

Gambas al Ajillo

Ingredients:

- 1 lb shrimp, peeled and deveined
- 4 cloves garlic, thinly sliced
- 1/4 cup olive oil
- 1 teaspoon red pepper flakes
- 1 tablespoon lemon juice
- Fresh parsley, chopped (for garnish)

Instructions:

1. **Heat Oil:** In a skillet, heat olive oil over medium heat. Add garlic and red pepper flakes, cooking until fragrant.
2. **Cook Shrimp:** Add shrimp to the skillet and cook for 2-3 minutes until pink.
3. **Add Lemon Juice:** Stir in lemon juice and garnish with parsley. Serve hot.

Pisto Manchego

Ingredients:

- 1 zucchini, diced
- 1 eggplant, diced
- 1 green bell pepper, diced
- 1 red bell pepper, diced
- 1 onion, diced
- 3 ripe tomatoes, chopped
- 1/4 cup olive oil
- Salt and pepper

Instructions:

1. **Cook Vegetables:** Heat olive oil in a skillet. Sauté onion and peppers until softened. Add zucchini and eggplant, cooking until tender.
2. **Add Tomatoes:** Stir in tomatoes and simmer for 20 minutes. Season with salt and pepper.
3. **Serve:** Serve as a side dish or with crusty bread.

Albondigas

Ingredients:

- 1 lb ground beef or pork
- 1/4 cup breadcrumbs
- 1 egg
- 2 cloves garlic, minced
- 1/4 cup onion, finely chopped
- 1 teaspoon paprika
- 1/2 teaspoon cumin
- 2 cups tomato sauce
- Olive oil
- Salt and pepper

Instructions:

1. **Make Meatballs:** In a bowl, mix ground meat, breadcrumbs, egg, garlic, onion, paprika, cumin, salt, and pepper. Form into small meatballs.
2. **Fry Meatballs:** Heat olive oil in a skillet and fry the meatballs until browned.
3. **Simmer in Sauce:** Add tomato sauce to the skillet and simmer for 15-20 minutes. Serve hot.

Fabada Asturiana

Ingredients:

- 2 cups dried white beans (soaked overnight)
- 1 chorizo sausage
- 1 morcilla (blood sausage)
- 1/4 lb pancetta
- 2 cloves garlic
- 1 onion, halved
- 1 teaspoon paprika
- Salt

Instructions:

1. **Cook Beans:** Drain soaked beans and place in a pot with garlic, onion, and pancetta. Cover with water and simmer for 1 hour.
2. **Add Sausages:** Add chorizo, morcilla, and paprika. Cook for another hour.
3. **Serve:** Remove sausages and slice before serving with the beans.

Pollo al Ajillo

Ingredients:

- 1 whole chicken, cut into pieces
- 6 cloves garlic, crushed
- 1/4 cup olive oil
- 1/4 cup white wine
- 1 teaspoon paprika
- Salt and pepper
- Fresh parsley, chopped (for garnish)

Instructions:

1. **Brown Chicken:** Heat olive oil in a skillet. Brown the chicken pieces on all sides.
2. **Add Garlic:** Add crushed garlic and cook until fragrant.
3. **Deglaze:** Pour in white wine and stir, scraping up any browned bits. Add paprika, salt, and pepper.
4. **Simmer:** Cover and cook on low heat for 25-30 minutes until chicken is tender.
5. **Serve:** Garnish with parsley and serve hot.

Calamares a la Romana

Ingredients:

- 1 lb squid, cleaned and cut into rings
- 1 cup all-purpose flour
- 2 large eggs, beaten
- 1 cup breadcrumbs
- 1 cup olive oil (for frying)
- Lemon wedges (for serving)
- Salt

Instructions:

1. **Prepare Squid:** Pat the squid rings dry and season with salt.
2. **Coat Squid:** Dredge each ring in flour, dip in beaten eggs, and coat with breadcrumbs.
3. **Fry:** Heat olive oil in a deep skillet and fry the squid rings until golden and crispy.
4. **Serve:** Drain on paper towels and serve with lemon wedges.

Escalivada

Ingredients:

- 2 eggplants
- 2 red bell peppers
- 2 onions
- 3 large tomatoes
- 1/4 cup olive oil
- Salt and pepper
- Optional: Anchovies (for garnish)

Instructions:

1. **Roast Vegetables:** Preheat oven to 400°F (200°C). Roast eggplants, peppers, onions, and tomatoes on a baking tray for 40-50 minutes, turning occasionally, until charred and soft.
2. **Peel and Slice:** Let the vegetables cool slightly, then peel and slice into strips.
3. **Season:** Arrange on a plate, drizzle with olive oil, and season with salt and pepper. Garnish with anchovies if desired.

Bacalao al Pil Pil

Ingredients:

- 4 pieces of salt cod, desalted
- 4 cloves garlic, sliced
- 1/2 cup olive oil
- 1 teaspoon chili flakes
- Fresh parsley (for garnish)

Instructions:

1. **Prepare Cod:** Rinse and pat the cod dry.
2. **Cook Garlic:** Heat olive oil in a skillet. Sauté garlic slices until golden and remove from the pan.
3. **Cook Cod:** Place cod in the skillet, skin side down. Cook on low heat, shaking the pan gently to create an emulsion with the oil.
4. **Serve:** Top with garlic, chili flakes, and parsley.

Churros con Chocolate

Ingredients:
For Churros:

- 1 cup water
- 1/4 cup unsalted butter
- 1 tablespoon sugar
- 1 cup all-purpose flour
- 2 large eggs
- Vegetable oil (for frying)
- Sugar and cinnamon (for coating)

For Chocolate Sauce:

- 4 oz dark chocolate
- 1 cup milk
- 1 tablespoon sugar

Instructions:

1. **Make Churro Dough:** Heat water, butter, and sugar in a saucepan until boiling. Remove from heat, stir in flour, and mix until smooth. Let cool slightly, then beat in eggs.
2. **Fry Churros:** Pipe dough into hot oil using a star tip and fry until golden. Roll in cinnamon sugar.
3. **Make Chocolate Sauce:** Melt chocolate with milk and sugar in a saucepan. Stir until smooth.
4. **Serve:** Serve churros with the chocolate sauce.

Jamón Ibérico Croquettes

Ingredients:

- 1/2 cup finely chopped Jamón Ibérico
- 1/4 cup unsalted butter
- 1/2 cup flour
- 1 1/2 cups milk
- Salt and pepper
- 2 eggs, beaten
- 1 cup breadcrumbs
- Olive oil (for frying)

Instructions:

1. **Make Filling:** Melt butter in a pan, stir in flour, and cook for 1 minute. Gradually add milk, whisking until thick. Stir in Jamón Ibérico, season, and cool.
2. **Shape Croquettes:** Shape the mixture into small logs, coat in flour, dip in eggs, and roll in breadcrumbs.
3. **Fry:** Heat olive oil and fry croquettes until golden.

Empanada Gallega

Ingredients:

- 2 sheets of puff pastry
- 1/2 lb tuna (or cooked chicken)
- 1 onion, finely chopped
- 1 red bell pepper, diced
- 1 cup tomato sauce
- Olive oil
- Salt and pepper
- 1 egg, beaten

Instructions:

1. **Make Filling:** Sauté onion and bell pepper in olive oil until softened. Stir in tuna (or chicken) and tomato sauce. Cook for 5 minutes and season.
2. **Assemble:** Place one puff pastry sheet on a baking tray, spread filling evenly, and cover with the second sheet. Seal edges.
3. **Bake:** Brush with beaten egg and bake at 375°F (190°C) for 25-30 minutes.

Salmorejo

Ingredients:

- 6 ripe tomatoes
- 1 clove garlic
- 1 cup stale bread, soaked in water
- 1/4 cup olive oil
- 2 tablespoons sherry vinegar
- Salt
- Hard-boiled egg and Jamón Ibérico (for garnish)

Instructions:

1. **Blend Ingredients:** Blend tomatoes, garlic, bread, olive oil, and vinegar until smooth. Season with salt.
2. **Chill:** Refrigerate for at least 1 hour.
3. **Serve:** Top with chopped egg and Jamón Ibérico.

Arroz Negro

Ingredients:

- 2 cups Bomba rice
- 4 cups fish stock
- 1/2 lb squid, cleaned and cut
- 1/4 cup olive oil
- 1 onion, finely chopped
- 1 clove garlic, minced
- 2 tablespoons squid ink
- Salt and pepper
- Lemon wedges (for serving)

Instructions:

1. **Sauté Ingredients:** Heat olive oil in a pan, sauté onion and garlic. Add squid and cook until tender.
2. **Cook Rice:** Stir in rice and squid ink. Add fish stock and simmer for 20 minutes.
3. **Serve:** Garnish with lemon wedges.

Pulpo a la Gallega

Ingredients:

- 1 whole octopus (about 2 lbs)
- 4 potatoes, sliced
- 1/4 cup olive oil
- 1 teaspoon paprika
- Salt

Instructions:

1. **Cook Octopus:** Boil octopus in salted water until tender (about 1 hour). Remove and let cool.
2. **Boil Potatoes:** In the same water, boil potato slices until tender.
3. **Serve:** Arrange potatoes on a plate, top with octopus slices, drizzle with olive oil, and sprinkle with paprika and salt.

Tarta de Santiago

Ingredients:

- 2 cups almond flour
- 1 cup granulated sugar
- 4 large eggs
- Zest of 1 lemon
- 1 teaspoon cinnamon
- Powdered sugar (for dusting)

Instructions:

1. **Preheat Oven:** Preheat to 350°F (175°C) and grease a round cake pan.
2. **Mix Batter:** In a bowl, mix almond flour, sugar, eggs, lemon zest, and cinnamon until smooth.
3. **Bake:** Pour into the pan and bake for 30-35 minutes.
4. **Decorate:** Let cool, then dust with powdered sugar, using a stencil of the Cross of St. James for authenticity.

Espinacas con Garbanzos

Ingredients:

- 2 cups cooked chickpeas
- 10 oz fresh spinach
- 2 cloves garlic, minced
- 2 tablespoons olive oil
- 1 teaspoon paprika
- 1/2 teaspoon cumin
- Salt and pepper
- 1 slice of bread (optional)

Instructions:

1. **Sauté Bread and Garlic:** Heat olive oil in a pan, fry the bread until golden, then remove. Sauté garlic until fragrant.
2. **Add Chickpeas and Spices:** Add chickpeas, paprika, and cumin. Cook for 5 minutes.
3. **Add Spinach:** Stir in spinach and cook until wilted. Mash the bread into crumbs and mix in if desired.
4. **Serve:** Season with salt and pepper.

Lentejas a la Riojana

Ingredients:

- 2 cups lentils
- 1 chorizo sausage, sliced
- 1 onion, chopped
- 1 carrot, diced
- 1 potato, diced
- 2 cloves garlic, minced
- 4 cups water or broth
- 1 teaspoon paprika
- Salt and pepper

Instructions:

1. **Sauté Vegetables:** In a pot, sauté onion, carrot, and garlic in olive oil.
2. **Add Lentils and Chorizo:** Stir in lentils, chorizo, and paprika.
3. **Simmer:** Add water or broth, bring to a boil, then reduce heat and simmer for 30-40 minutes.
4. **Season:** Add potato halfway through cooking. Season with salt and pepper.

Fideuà

Ingredients:

- 2 cups short pasta (fideos or vermicelli)
- 1/2 lb seafood (shrimp, squid, mussels)
- 1 onion, diced
- 2 cloves garlic, minced
- 2 cups fish stock
- 2 tomatoes, grated
- 1/4 cup olive oil
- Saffron threads (optional)
- Lemon wedges (for serving)

Instructions:

1. **Toast Pasta:** Heat olive oil in a pan, add pasta, and toast until golden. Remove and set aside.
2. **Cook Seafood:** Sauté onion, garlic, and seafood until fragrant. Add grated tomatoes and cook for 5 minutes.
3. **Simmer:** Stir in stock and saffron. Return pasta to the pan and cook until liquid is absorbed.
4. **Serve:** Garnish with lemon wedges.

Cocido Madrileño

Ingredients:

- 1 lb chickpeas, soaked overnight
- 1/2 lb beef shank
- 1/2 lb chicken
- 1 chorizo sausage
- 1 morcilla (blood sausage)
- 1 ham bone
- 2 potatoes, peeled and diced
- 1 cabbage, chopped
- 2 carrots, peeled and sliced
- Salt

Instructions:

1. **Cook Meats and Chickpeas:** In a large pot, boil chickpeas, beef, chicken, chorizo, morcilla, and ham bone for 2 hours. Skim off foam.
2. **Add Vegetables:** Add potatoes, cabbage, and carrots. Simmer for another hour.
3. **Serve:** Serve the broth as a soup, followed by chickpeas and meats as the main course.

Caldereta de Cordero

Ingredients:

- 1 lb lamb, cubed
- 1 onion, diced
- 2 tomatoes, grated
- 2 cloves garlic, minced
- 2 potatoes, cubed
- 1/2 cup white wine
- 2 cups water or broth
- 1/4 cup olive oil
- 1 teaspoon paprika
- 1 bay leaf
- Salt and pepper

Instructions:

1. **Brown Lamb:** Heat olive oil in a pot, brown the lamb, and set aside.
2. **Sauté Vegetables:** Sauté onion, garlic, and tomatoes in the same pot.
3. **Simmer:** Return lamb to the pot, add potatoes, wine, water, paprika, bay leaf, salt, and pepper. Simmer for 40-50 minutes.

Chistorra al Vino

Ingredients:

- 1 lb chistorra sausage
- 1 cup white wine
- 1 tablespoon olive oil

Instructions:

1. **Cook Sausage:** Heat olive oil in a pan and brown the chistorra.
2. **Add Wine:** Pour in wine and simmer until reduced by half.
3. **Serve:** Serve hot with crusty bread.

Huevos a la Flamenca

Ingredients:

- 4 eggs
- 1 cup tomato sauce
- 1/2 cup peas
- 1/2 cup diced ham
- 1/4 cup olive oil
- 1 red bell pepper, sliced
- Salt and pepper

Instructions:

1. **Prepare Sauce:** Heat olive oil in a skillet, add tomato sauce, peas, ham, and bell pepper. Cook for 5 minutes.
2. **Add Eggs:** Make wells in the sauce, crack an egg into each, and cover. Cook until eggs are set.
3. **Serve:** Serve hot with crusty bread.

Ensalada Rusa

Ingredients:

- 3 potatoes, boiled and diced
- 2 carrots, boiled and diced
- 1 cup peas, boiled
- 1/2 cup mayonnaise
- 1 can tuna, drained
- Salt and pepper

Instructions:

1. **Combine Ingredients:** Mix potatoes, carrots, peas, tuna, and mayonnaise in a bowl.
2. **Season:** Add salt and pepper to taste.
3. **Chill and Serve:** Refrigerate before serving.

Merluza a la Koskera

Ingredients:

- 4 hake fillets
- 1/2 cup olive oil
- 2 garlic cloves, minced
- 1/2 cup white wine
- 1/2 cup fish stock
- 1/2 cup green peas
- 8 white asparagus spears (canned or fresh)
- 8 clams
- Fresh parsley, chopped

Instructions:

1. **Sauté Garlic:** Heat olive oil in a pan, add garlic, and sauté until fragrant.
2. **Cook Hake:** Add hake fillets and cook on medium heat for 2 minutes per side.
3. **Simmer Sauce:** Pour in wine and stock. Add peas, asparagus, and clams. Cover and cook until clams open.
4. **Serve:** Sprinkle with parsley and serve hot.

Rabo de Toro

Ingredients:

- 2 lbs oxtail, cut into pieces
- 1 onion, chopped
- 2 carrots, sliced
- 2 tomatoes, grated
- 2 cloves garlic, minced
- 1 cup red wine
- 2 cups beef stock
- 1 bay leaf
- Olive oil
- Salt and pepper

Instructions:

1. **Brown Oxtail:** Heat olive oil in a pot, brown oxtail pieces, and set aside.
2. **Sauté Vegetables:** In the same pot, sauté onion, carrot, and garlic. Add tomatoes and cook for 5 minutes.
3. **Simmer:** Add oxtail, wine, stock, bay leaf, salt, and pepper. Cover and simmer for 2-3 hours until tender.
4. **Serve:** Serve with crusty bread or mashed potatoes.

Callos a la Madrileña

Ingredients:

- 2 lbs beef tripe, cleaned and cut into pieces
- 1 chorizo sausage, sliced
- 1 morcilla (blood sausage), sliced
- 1 onion, chopped
- 2 garlic cloves, minced
- 1 teaspoon paprika
- 1 bay leaf
- 2 cups beef stock
- Olive oil
- Salt

Instructions:

1. **Prepare Tripe:** Boil tripe in water for 10 minutes, then drain.
2. **Sauté Onion and Garlic:** Heat olive oil in a pot, sauté onion and garlic. Add paprika and stir.
3. **Simmer:** Add tripe, chorizo, morcilla, bay leaf, and stock. Cover and simmer for 1-2 hours until tender.
4. **Serve:** Serve hot with bread.

Zarzuela de Pescado

Ingredients:

- 1 lb mixed seafood (fish, shrimp, clams, squid)
- 1 onion, chopped
- 2 tomatoes, grated
- 2 garlic cloves, minced
- 1/2 cup white wine
- 1/2 cup fish stock
- Olive oil
- Salt and pepper

Instructions:

1. **Sauté Onion and Garlic:** Heat olive oil in a pan, sauté onion and garlic. Add tomatoes and cook for 5 minutes.
2. **Add Seafood:** Add seafood, wine, and stock. Cover and simmer until seafood is cooked.
3. **Season:** Season with salt and pepper, then serve with crusty bread.

Migas Extremeñas

Ingredients:

- 1 lb day-old bread, cubed
- 1/4 cup olive oil
- 4 cloves garlic, minced
- 1 chorizo sausage, sliced
- 1/4 cup diced pancetta
- Paprika
- Salt

Instructions:

1. **Moisten Bread:** Lightly sprinkle bread cubes with water to moisten.
2. **Cook Garlic and Meats:** Heat olive oil in a pan, sauté garlic, chorizo, and pancetta.
3. **Add Bread:** Add bread and paprika. Stir and cook until crispy.
4. **Serve:** Serve hot as a snack or side dish.

Pimientos del Piquillo Rellenos

Ingredients:

- 8 piquillo peppers (canned or fresh)
- 1 cup cooked and shredded cod or chicken
- 1/2 cup béchamel sauce
- Olive oil
- Salt

Instructions:

1. **Prepare Filling:** Mix cod or chicken with béchamel sauce.
2. **Stuff Peppers:** Fill peppers with the mixture.
3. **Cook:** Place in a baking dish, drizzle with olive oil, and bake at 350°F (175°C) for 15 minutes.
4. **Serve:** Serve warm.

Conejo al Salmorejo

Ingredients:

- 1 rabbit, cut into pieces
- 4 cloves garlic
- 1 teaspoon paprika
- 1/2 teaspoon cumin
- 1 cup white wine
- Olive oil
- Salt and pepper

Instructions:

1. **Marinate Rabbit:** Blend garlic, paprika, cumin, wine, salt, and pepper. Marinate rabbit pieces overnight.
2. **Cook Rabbit:** Heat olive oil in a pan, brown rabbit pieces, and add marinade. Cover and simmer for 30-40 minutes.
3. **Serve:** Serve with potatoes or salad.

Boquerones en Vinagre

Ingredients:

- 1 lb fresh anchovies, cleaned
- 1/2 cup white vinegar
- 2 tablespoons olive oil
- 2 garlic cloves, sliced
- Fresh parsley, chopped
- Salt

Instructions:

1. **Marinate Anchovies:** Layer anchovies in a dish, cover with vinegar, and refrigerate for 4-6 hours.
2. **Dress:** Drain vinegar, drizzle with olive oil, and top with garlic and parsley.
3. **Serve:** Serve cold as a tapa.

Berenjenas con Miel

Ingredients:

- 2 eggplants, sliced
- 1 cup flour
- Olive oil for frying
- Honey or molasses
- Salt

Instructions:

1. **Prepare Eggplant:** Soak slices in salted water for 30 minutes, then pat dry.
2. **Fry:** Coat in flour and fry in hot olive oil until golden.
3. **Serve:** Drizzle with honey or molasses before serving.

Chuletas de Cordero a la Manchega

Ingredients:

- 8 lamb chops
- 1/4 cup olive oil
- 2 cloves garlic, minced
- 1 teaspoon rosemary
- Salt and pepper

Instructions:

1. **Marinate Lamb:** Marinate chops with olive oil, garlic, rosemary, salt, and pepper for 1 hour.
2. **Cook:** Grill or pan-fry chops until golden and cooked to your liking.
3. **Serve:** Serve with roasted vegetables or potatoes.

Almejas a la Marinera

Ingredients:

- 2 lbs clams
- 2 tablespoons olive oil
- 1 onion, finely chopped
- 2 garlic cloves, minced
- 1 cup white wine
- 1/2 cup tomato sauce
- 1 teaspoon paprika
- Fresh parsley, chopped
- Salt

Instructions:

1. **Clean Clams:** Soak clams in salted water for 1 hour, then rinse thoroughly.
2. **Sauté Aromatics:** Heat olive oil in a pan, sauté onion and garlic until softened.
3. **Simmer Sauce:** Add wine, tomato sauce, and paprika. Simmer for 5 minutes.
4. **Cook Clams:** Add clams, cover, and cook until they open (discard any that remain closed).
5. **Serve:** Garnish with parsley and serve with crusty bread.

Arroz con Leche

Ingredients:

- 1 cup short-grain rice
- 4 cups whole milk
- 1 cup sugar
- 1 cinnamon stick
- Lemon peel (from 1 lemon)
- Ground cinnamon (for garnish)

Instructions:

1. **Cook Rice:** In a pot, combine rice, milk, cinnamon stick, and lemon peel. Cook on low heat, stirring often, for 30 minutes.
2. **Add Sugar:** Stir in sugar and cook for another 10 minutes until creamy.
3. **Cool:** Remove from heat, discard cinnamon stick and lemon peel. Let cool.
4. **Serve:** Garnish with ground cinnamon and serve chilled or at room temperature.

Solomillo al Whisky

Ingredients:

- 1 lb pork tenderloin, sliced into medallions
- 4 garlic cloves, sliced
- 1/2 cup olive oil
- 1/2 cup whisky
- 1/2 cup chicken stock
- Lemon juice (from 1 lemon)
- Salt and pepper

Instructions:

1. **Cook Pork:** Heat olive oil in a pan, season pork with salt and pepper, and cook until golden. Remove and set aside.
2. **Sauté Garlic:** In the same pan, sauté garlic until golden.
3. **Deglaze:** Add whisky, lemon juice, and chicken stock. Simmer for 5 minutes.
4. **Combine:** Return pork to the pan, cook for 2-3 minutes.
5. **Serve:** Serve with potatoes or crusty bread.

Paté de Cabracho

Ingredients:

- 1 lb scorpionfish (or substitute cod)
- 4 eggs
- 1/2 cup heavy cream
- 1/2 cup tomato sauce
- 1/4 cup olive oil
- Salt and pepper

Instructions:

1. **Cook Fish:** Boil or steam the fish, remove bones, and flake the meat.
2. **Blend Ingredients:** In a blender, combine fish, eggs, cream, tomato sauce, olive oil, salt, and pepper. Blend until smooth.
3. **Bake:** Pour into a greased loaf pan and bake at 350°F (175°C) for 40 minutes.
4. **Serve:** Cool, slice, and serve with crackers or bread.

Cordero Asado a la Segoviana

Ingredients:

- 2 lbs lamb shoulder or leg
- 2 garlic cloves, minced
- 2 tablespoons olive oil
- 1/2 cup white wine
- 1/2 cup water
- Fresh rosemary
- Salt and pepper

Instructions:

1. **Prepare Lamb:** Rub lamb with garlic, olive oil, rosemary, salt, and pepper.
2. **Roast:** Place in a roasting pan with wine and water. Roast at 375°F (190°C) for 2 hours, basting occasionally.
3. **Serve:** Serve with roasted potatoes or salad.

Chanfaina

Ingredients:

- 1 lb lamb liver, kidney, or meat (cubed)
- 1 onion, chopped
- 1 green bell pepper, chopped
- 2 garlic cloves, minced
- 1 cup tomato sauce
- 1 teaspoon paprika
- Olive oil
- Salt and pepper

Instructions:

1. **Cook Meat:** Heat olive oil in a pan, cook lamb pieces until browned, and set aside.
2. **Sauté Vegetables:** In the same pan, sauté onion, pepper, and garlic.
3. **Simmer:** Add meat, tomato sauce, paprika, salt, and pepper. Simmer for 20-30 minutes.
4. **Serve:** Serve with rice or bread.

Bacalao a la Vizcaína

Ingredients:

- 1 lb salt cod, soaked overnight and desalted
- 1 onion, chopped
- 2 garlic cloves, minced
- 1 cup red peppers, roasted and pureed
- 1/2 cup tomato sauce
- 1/4 cup olive oil
- Salt

Instructions:

1. **Cook Cod:** Heat olive oil in a pan, add cod, and cook for 2 minutes per side. Remove and set aside.
2. **Prepare Sauce:** In the same pan, sauté onion and garlic. Add red pepper puree, tomato sauce, and a pinch of salt. Simmer for 10 minutes.
3. **Combine:** Return cod to the pan, cover, and cook for another 5 minutes.
4. **Serve:** Serve with boiled potatoes or crusty bread.

Chorizo a la Sidra

Ingredients:

- 1 lb Spanish chorizo (sliced)
- 1 cup cider (hard cider or sweet apple cider)

Instructions:

1. **Cook Chorizo:** Place chorizo slices in a skillet over medium heat. Cook until lightly browned.
2. **Add Cider:** Pour cider into the skillet, reduce heat, and simmer for 10-15 minutes until the cider reduces slightly.
3. **Serve:** Serve warm with crusty bread as a tapa.

Leche Frita

Ingredients:

- 2 cups whole milk
- 1/2 cup sugar
- 1/4 cup cornstarch
- 1 cinnamon stick
- Lemon peel (from 1 lemon)
- 1/2 cup flour (for coating)
- 1 egg (beaten)
- Oil (for frying)
- Cinnamon sugar (for dusting)

Instructions:

1. **Prepare Custard:** Heat milk with cinnamon stick and lemon peel. Remove from heat and let steep. Mix sugar and cornstarch, then whisk into strained milk. Cook over low heat until thickened.
2. **Chill:** Pour custard into a greased dish, let cool, and refrigerate until firm.
3. **Fry:** Cut into squares, coat with flour and egg, and fry until golden.
4. **Dust:** Sprinkle with cinnamon sugar and serve.

Mejillones al Vapor

Ingredients:

- 2 lbs fresh mussels
- 1/2 cup white wine
- 2 garlic cloves, minced
- 2 tablespoons olive oil
- Fresh parsley, chopped

Instructions:

1. **Clean Mussels:** Scrub mussels and remove beards.
2. **Steam:** In a large pot, heat olive oil, add garlic, and sauté for 1 minute. Add wine and mussels, cover, and steam until mussels open (discard any that remain closed).
3. **Serve:** Sprinkle with parsley and serve with lemon wedges.

Revuelto de Setas

Ingredients:

- 2 cups mixed wild mushrooms (cleaned and sliced)
- 4 eggs
- 2 tablespoons olive oil
- 1 garlic clove, minced
- Salt and pepper
- Fresh parsley, chopped

Instructions:

1. **Cook Mushrooms:** Heat olive oil in a skillet, add garlic, and sauté. Add mushrooms and cook until tender.
2. **Add Eggs:** Beat eggs with salt and pepper, pour over mushrooms, and cook gently, stirring, until just set.
3. **Serve:** Garnish with parsley and serve immediately.

Tumbet

Ingredients:

- 1 large eggplant (sliced)
- 2 zucchini (sliced)
- 2 potatoes (sliced)
- 1 cup tomato sauce
- 1/4 cup olive oil
- Salt

Instructions:

1. **Fry Vegetables:** Heat olive oil in a pan. Fry eggplant, zucchini, and potatoes separately until golden. Drain on paper towels.
2. **Layer:** In a baking dish, layer potatoes, zucchini, and eggplant. Top with tomato sauce.
3. **Bake:** Bake at 350°F (175°C) for 20 minutes.
4. **Serve:** Serve warm or at room temperature.

Torrijas

Ingredients:

- 1 loaf stale bread (sliced)
- 2 cups milk
- 1/2 cup sugar
- Lemon peel (from 1 lemon)
- 1 cinnamon stick
- 2 eggs (beaten)
- Oil (for frying)
- Cinnamon sugar (for dusting)

Instructions:

1. **Infuse Milk:** Heat milk with sugar, cinnamon stick, and lemon peel. Let cool.
2. **Soak Bread:** Dip bread slices into infused milk, then coat with beaten eggs.
3. **Fry:** Fry in hot oil until golden brown. Drain on paper towels.
4. **Dust:** Sprinkle with cinnamon sugar and serve warm

www.ingramcontent.com/pod-product-compliance
Lightning Source LLC
LaVergne TN
LVHW081505060526
838201LV00056BA/2942